Hugs

We all love hugs, and lots of animals love hugs too!

When you give a hug, you get one right back.

That's why hugging makes cuddly creatures feel safe, relaxed, warm and happy.

We love to hold each other **tight.**
We playfight and then we **hug** to show we are still **friends.**

Young elephants love to play. Like many other young animals, they pretend to fight and they enjoy the rough and tumble of playtime.

This is my dad's big belly hug! I love his warm and cosy cuddles.

Emperor penguins live near the South Pole and have to survive snow, ice and freezing winds. A chick sits on its father's feet, and his fluffy belly blanket keeps it warm.

I love to **hug**.
I feel safe when I hug my **mum**.
I know she will look after **me**.

When a lemur baby is born it holds on to its mother's belly. When the baby is old enough, it holds on to its mother's back as she leaps between trees.

The best hugs are big bear hugs.

A polar bear mother normally has two cubs at a time, and she will fight to protect them. The cubs play together to exercise, and to learn how to hunt.

We love
to cuddle
at bedtime.
It's easy to
fall asleep
when you
know someone
loves you.

Sea otters spend most of their
lives at sea, and they often hold
hands when they sleep. Baby otters
are called pups and their mothers
hold them on their tummies.

When a friend is feeling sad, just wrap your arms around them and gently squeeze.

Northern white-cheeked gibbons can change colour. They are all born cream but turn black when they are about two years old. Females then turn cream again.

The world isn't so scary when you've got someone to hug.

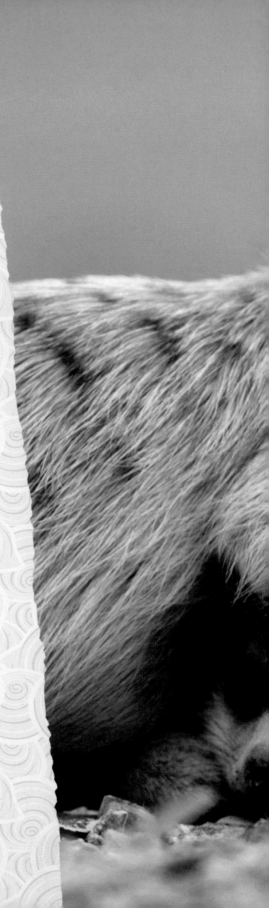

Meerkats live in big, friendly family groups. They live in burrows but come to the surface to look for food. Meerkats stand guard near their burrows, and look out for danger.

We love to
hug trees!
We are brothers,
and holding hands
makes us feel all
warm inside.

Mother raccoons have babies
once a year. They have three
to seven babies at a time,
and they look after them in
dens they have built in trees.

My dad gives me cuddles. It's his way of showing me just how much he cares.

A father lion looks after his cubs when the mothers go hunting. The cubs often pester their dad, but he gently pushes them away if they get too annoying!

We love to snuggle up.

We call this hug a buddy body blanket!

It is often cold and snowy in the places where Japanese macaques live. They keep warm by bathing in natural hot water springs, and by cuddling!

I know my mum loves me because she wraps her arms around me and tells me so.

Chimps are our closest relatives, so it is no wonder they like to hug as much as we do. They also like to play, be tickled and kissed!

Mum's asleep, but I can still sneak in for a quick snuggle...

Taking care of newborn cubs is hard work. They are blind and helpless, so their mother must do everything for them. Tiger cubs begin to hunt when they are six months old.

We love a group hug! Everyone can join in...

Orang-utan babies stay with their mother until they are about ten years old. Baby orang-utans love to play, hold hands, hug and kiss.

A hug is worth a hundred words. We don't need to talk when we hold each other tight.

Newborn panda bears are tiny and they weigh about the same as an apple. At first, a cub feeds on its mother's milk. Later it will learn how to find and eat bamboo.

Here are three good reasons for hugging.

A cuddle is a good way to show someone you love them.

♥

A snuggle makes you feel safe and warm.

♥

A hug is worth a hundred words...

Can you think of any more?

Editor: Tasha Percy
Designer: Natalie Godwin

Copyright © QED Publishing 2014

First published in the UK in 2014 by
QED Publishing
A Quarto Group company
The Old Brewery, 6 Blundell Street
London, N7 9BH

www.qed-publishing.co.uk

A catalogue record for this book is available from the British Library.

ISBN 978 1 78171 556 7

Printed in China

Picture credits
(t=top, b=bottom, l=left, r=right, c=centre, fc=front cover)
1c: naturepl.com: Eric Baccega, 2c: Foto Natura: Flip De Nooyer, 3r: Shutterstock:
Background, 4l: Shutterstock: Background, 5r: naturepl.com: Tony Heald, 6c: Frans
Lanting Stock: Frans Lanting, 7r: istockphoto.com: Background, 8l: Shutterstock:
Background, 9r: naturepl.com: Anup Shah, 10c: FLPA: ImageBroker, 11r: istockphoto.
com: Background, 12l: Shutterstock: Background, 13c: FLPA: Suzi Eszterhas, 14c:
FLPA: Christian Hütter, 15r: Shutterstock: Background, 16l: istockphoto.com:
Background, 17r Getty Images; (c) Paul Souders, 18c: Minden Pictures: Tim Fitzharris,
19r: Shutterstock: Background, 20l: Shutterstock: Background, 21c: Minden Pictures:
Suzi Eszterhas, 22c: Foto Natura: Stephen Belcher, 23r: Shutterstock: Background, 24l:
istockphoto.com: Background, 25r: Corbis: © Frans Lanting, 26l: FLPA: Suzi Eszterhas,
27r: Shutterstock: Background, 28l: Shutterstock: Background, 29r: FLPA: Mitsuaki
Iwago, 30l: ZSSD, 31r: Shutterstock: Background, 32c: Shutterstock: Background, tl:
© Biosphoto: Michel & Christine